Proclaiming the Risen Lord

Luke 24 – Acts 2

by Peter Bolt

matthiasmedia

Proclaiming the Risen Lord

Published in the United Kingdom by:
The Good Book Company Ltd
Elm House, 37 Elm Road
New Malden, Surrey KT3 3HB
Tel: 0845 225 0880; Fax: 0845 225 0990
email: admin@thegoodbook.co.uk
website: www.thegoodbook.co.uk

ISBN 1 876326 98 0

Printed in China

Contents

How to make the most of these studies

1. What is an interactive Bible Study?

These 'interactive' Bible studies are a bit like a guided tour of a famous city. The studies will take you through a key theme of Luke and Acts, that is, the proclamation of the gospel, pointing out things along the way, filling in background details, and suggesting avenues for further exploration. But there is also time for you to do some sight-seeing of your own—to wander off, have a good look for yourself, and form your own conclusions.

In other words, we have designed these studies to fall half-way between a sermon and a set of unadorned Bible study questions. We want to provide stimulation and input and point you in the right direction, leaving you to do a lot of the exploration and study yourself.

We hope that these studies will stimulate lots of 'interaction'—interaction with the Bible, with the things we've written, with your own current thoughts and attitudes, with other people as you discuss them, and with God as you talk to him about it all.

2. The format

Each study contains sections of text to introduce, summarize, suggest and provoke. We've left plenty of room in the margins for you to jot comments and questions as you read.

Interspersed throughout the text are two types of 'interaction', each with its own symbol:

Investigate

Questions to help you investigate key parts of the Bible.

Think it through

Questions to help you think through the implications of your discoveries and write down your thoughts and reactions.

When you come to one of these symbols, you'll know that it's time to do some work of your own.

3. Suggestions for individual study

- Before you begin, pray that God would open your eyes to what he is saying in the Bible, and give you the spiritual strength to do something about it. You may be spurred to pray again at the end of the study.
- Work through the study, following the directions as you go. Write in the spaces provided.
- Resist the temptation to skip over the *Think it through* sections. It is important to think about the sections of text (rather than just accepting them as true) and to ponder the implications for your life. Writing these things down is a very valuable way to get your thoughts working.
- Take what opportunities you can to talk to others about what you've learnt.

4. Suggestions for group study

- Much of the above applies to group study as well. The studies are suitable for structured Bible study or cell groups, as well as for more informal pairs and threesomes. Get together with a friend/s and work through them at your own pace; use them as the basis for regular Bible study with your spouse. You don't need the formal structure of a 'group' to gain maximum benefit.
- It is *vital* that group members work through the study themselves *before* the group meets. The group discussion can take place comfortably in an hour (depending on how sidetracked you get!), but only if all the members have done the work and are familiar with the material.
- Spend most of the group time discussing the 'interactive' sections—*Investigate* and *Think it through*. Reading all the text together will take too long and should be unnecessary if the group members have done their preparation. You may wish to underline and read aloud particular paragraphs or sections of text that you think are important.
- The role of the group leader is to direct the course of the discussion and to try to draw the threads together at the end. This will mean a little extra preparation—underlining important sections of text to emphasize, working out which questions are worth concentrating on, and being sure of the main thrust of the study. Leaders will also probably want to work out approximately how long they'd like to spend on each part.
- We haven't included an 'answer guide' to the questions in the studies. This is a deliberate move. We want to give you a guided tour of the theme of proclamation of the gospel in Luke and Acts, not a lecture. There is more than enough in the text we have written and the questions we have asked to point you in what we think is the right direction. The rest is up to you.

5. Bible translation

Previous studies in our Interactive Bible Study series have assumed that most readers would be using the New International Version of the Bible. However, since the release of the English Standard Version in 2001, many have switched to the ESV for study purposes. For this reason, we have decided to quote from and refer to the ESV text, which we recommend.

1

Luke 24 v 13-27

The Proclaimer and his proclamation

Since the beginning, Christians have been proclaiming the good news about Jesus Christ. Well, 'proclaiming' might sound a little formal. For sure, there are plenty of formal occasions when such proclamation occurs. But Christianity has always been a grass roots movement. The proclamation of the good news has happened in many settings, both formal and informal, with Christian people chatting the news about Jesus wherever they happen to be and to whomever they happen to be speaking. Christian proclamation runs across the face of the earth (cf. 2 Thess 3:1) as it follows the lines of our relationships and contacts with other people.

But in the end, who is doing the proclamation? It is a wonderful thing to realize that although we are the ones speaking about Jesus, it is actually *Jesus* who is speaking through us. *He* is the ultimate proclaimer of this message. We are simply his mouthpieces.

Investigate

Read Luke 24:13-27.

1. What startling events had taken place in Jerusalem?

2. Why were the disciples disappointed (v. 21)? (Cf. Luke 1:67-79)

3. Why did the two disciples fail to understand what had taken place?

4. What two things did the Scriptures predict about the Christ? How do these two things relate to the events in Jerusalem?

Jesus is risen!

Luke has already told the story of Jesus' death (Luke 23), and now he tells the story of Jesus' resurrection from the dead (Luke 24). These are the events that launch the time of proclamation. The resurrection of Jesus is especially important in this regard.

For centuries, Christians have confessed a most remarkable event as the central part of their belief: a man has risen from the dead! Towards the end of the book of Acts, when Paul was on trial before a series of authorities, he was given the opportunity to summarize the Christian message. When he did so, he said that he was on trial for the resurrection of the dead (Acts 23:6-8; 24:20-21). It was part of mainstream Jewish hope that one day, at the end of time, God would raise the dead from their graves (Dan 12:1-2). Paul and the other early Christians proclaimed that this last-day resurrection had already begun in the present time with one man: Jesus Christ had risen from the dead (see Acts 4:2 and 26:6-8). Jesus Christ was "the first to rise from the dead" (Acts 26:23).

But what do we mean when we say, 'Jesus rose from the dead'?

Investigate

Refer once again to Luke 24:13-27. This time, we are looking for the evidence that gave rise to the belief in the resurrection of Jesus.

1. What three things had happened that amazed the disciples (vv. 21b-24)?

2. What was happening to them at this very moment that also demonstrated the reality of the resurrection of Jesus?

3. What other evidence is presented in the chapter (vv. 33-34; 36-43)?

4. Why do you think Luke gives all the details in verses 37-43? (See also Acts 10:41-42.)

The belief in Jesus' resurrection arises from two collections of first-century events. First, the grave in which his body was laid was found to be empty. Secondly, the risen Jesus appeared to many people, giving "many proofs" (Acts 1:3) that he was the one who was crucified, but has now risen from the dead.

This is such an incredible event that it is really no surprise at all that people have found it difficult to accept. Dead people do not normally rise from the dead—this phenomenon is unknown to ordinary human experience. But the Christian message recognizes this and proclaims that this was not an ordinary event, because Jesus was not an ordinary man. He was the Christ, and the Scriptures had predicted that the Christ would suffer and then enter into his glory (Luke 24:26).

There have been sceptics, since the early days, who have had a great deal of difficulty with the resurrection of Jesus. Some have been happier to talk about some kind of spiritual resurrection, in which the body of Jesus did not leave the tomb. But this is not the view put forward by Luke. He stresses the fact that the body was not found in the tomb. He provides details that show the disciples discovering that the body of the risen Christ was the flesh and bones of the once crucified and buried Jesus. The empty tomb and the appearances meld together to point towards one conclusion: Jesus Christ has risen from the dead!

This too is consistent with him being 'the Christ'. This is the message proclaimed by Peter and Paul in their first-recorded sermons in Acts. When Peter stands before the assembled crowd in Jerusalem at Pentecost, he reminds them of the prophecy of Psalm 16, that God would not allow his 'Holy One' to see decay. Now this clearly could not apply to David, Peter says, because great though David was, he died and was buried and "his tomb is with us to this day" (Acts 2:29). Not so with Jesus:

> "... he was not abandoned to Hades, nor did his flesh see corruption. This Jesus God raised up, and of that we all are witnesses. Being therefore exalted at the right hand of God, and having received from the Father the promise of the Holy Spirit, he has poured out this that you yourselves are seeing and hearing. For David did not ascend into the heavens, but he himself says,
>
> 'The Lord said to my Lord, Sit at my right hand,
> until I make your enemies your footstool.'
>
> Let all the house of Israel therefore know for certain that God has made him both Lord and Christ, this Jesus whom you crucified." (Acts 2:31-36)

The risen Christ becomes the Proclaimer

The fact that a man rose from the dead is certainly worth speaking about in its own right. But there is another reason why the resurrection of Jesus resulted in the great time of proclamation being launched on the world. The risen Christ himself is the one doing the proclamation!

Investigate

Read the following verses. Who is the one taking all the initiative?

Luke 24:49; Acts 2:32-33

Acts 3:26

Acts 26:23

The Proclaimer behind our proclamation

The good news of Jesus Christ is certainly worth the telling. From the beginning, Christians have overflowed with that news. As they have believed the gospel, they have proclaimed, spoken and conversed the gospel to others (cf. 2 Cor 4:13).

But behind all this human speaking there is a far more powerful force at work. Jesus himself—the long-awaited Christ, now risen from the dead—is the one who proclaims this good news. As the first to rise from the dead, he now proclaims "light [to his own] people and to the Gentiles" (Acts 26:23).

Now, that is *some* backing!

Think it through

1. List the different networks of people that you come across in your life (e.g. family, sporting).

2. When you think about 'chatting the gospel' to these people, what are:

    a. the things that would make it hard?

    b. the things that would make it easy?

3. How has this study helped you think about the opportunities you have for proclamation among all these people?

2

Proclamation in God's plan

It has often been said that we find it difficult to distinguish the *important* from the *urgent*. Life in the twenty-first century can be extremely hectic. There are so many things that press in upon us, clamouring for our attention. There are so many *urgent* things that apparently *have* to be done.

But that doesn't mean that they are all *important*. In fact, the hectic pace of our lives can get in the way of what is truly important. It is increasingly recognized, for example, that the frantic pace of life in the western world can squeeze out other human beings, and the joys of human relationships are increasingly under threat of being lost. Recognizing the danger, we all realize that this is something *important* that is being swallowed by the tyranny of the *urgent*.

The proclamation of the good news of Jesus, however, is *both* urgent *and* important. It is *urgent* because of the times in which we live, and it is *important* because of the place it has in God's plans. Because proclamation of this good news is so *important* in God's plans, it also helps us to re-value all of the many aspects and priorities of our lives, and so it helps us deal with all those other urgent/important things.

Let's go back to our roots once again, to the launch of the age of proclamation.

Investigate

Read Luke 24:36-53.

1. What was it that Jesus wanted the disciples to understand (vv. 44-45)?

2. Why is an understanding of God's purposes and plans so important to human life?

3. What three things were predicted in the Scriptures of "the Christ" (vv. 46-47)? As Jesus is speaking, how many of these things have already been fulfilled?

4. What does this tell us about the times in which we live, that is, the times since the resurrection of the Christ?

God's plans for his world

Wouldn't be terrible if God left people in the dark about himself? If God stayed silent, and never showed himself, or spoke about himself, then there would be no clear knowledge of God's plans and purposes. Without knowledge of his plans, there would be no opportunity for us to seek to live our lives in the light of his plans—even if we wanted to! If God remained silent, then it would be anybody's guess what God's plans were for this world.

But, thankfully, that is not the situation that we have to put up with. In God's kindness, he has revealed himself and made his plans and purposes known. In the Old Testament, God spoke of what he would do one day. With the coming of Jesus Christ, the New Testament spoke of what he had done. Once we know what he has done, then we also know what he is doing in this world, and what he will do in our future.

Investigate

Read the following verses. What do they say about God's plans?

Luke 4:16-21

Luke 9:31, 9:51, 13:32-33; Acts 1:11

Acts 2:22-24

Acts 13:36-48

Acts 17:30-31

Jesus Christ: The centre of God's plans

Jesus is at the centre of God's plans. When he spoke with his disciples after the resurrection, he showed them how the Old Testament had spoken about him, and how it had predicted his death and resurrection (Luke 24:25-27; 24:44-47).

In fact, without understanding the Old Testament promises, it was impossible for them to understand the true significance of the strange events that had occurred in Jerusalem (see Luke 24:21, then 25). God had laid out his plans throughout many hundreds of years of Israel's history. And now, in the death and resurrection of the Christ, they had, at last, been fulfilled. Jesus Christ is at the climax and centre of God's plans.

In fact, because Jesus' death and resurrection are the climax of God's promises, these events brought a new era—a new time-period—to this world.

Investigate

Read Acts 2:14-21, 29-33.

1. How does Peter explain the gift of the Spirit on the day of Pentecost?

2. What is the blessing that is now available for "everyone who calls on the name of the Lord"? (See also vv. 37-41.)

3. How would you describe these "last days" (v. 17)? What (according to God's plans) are they *for*?

4. Is there any *urgency* about these "last days"? Why, or why not?

The risen Christ and the plan of God

From the beginning of his ministry, Jesus had proclaimed his message of salvation to all who would give him a hearing. Much of the Gospel of Luke shows him doing this work. On that dramatic day in Nazareth (Luke 4:16-21), he read out Isaiah 61 to the assembled people, and then announced that it had been fulfilled in their hearing. For about three years, Jesus continued to proclaim this message to the people of Israel.

After he rose again from the dead, the plan of God took a different turn.

Investigate

Recall Luke 24:45-47. What was the only thing in God's plan that had yet to be fulfilled?

Christ has risen from the dead; the nations of the world must now hear his good news. This is what God considers to be important. This is also what God considers to be urgent. This is the character of the times in which we live.

Think it through

1. How does the New Testament's 'last days' perspective compare to the perspective of the world around us?

2. Where do you notice the clash between these two world views most acutely? Provide some examples.

3. How does Luke's perspective on time help to sort out what is urgent and what is important in our own lives?

3 *The message proclaimed*

Jesus once said, "out of the abundance of the heart, [the evil person's] mouth speaks" (see Luke 6:43-45; cf. Rom 10:8-9). He also said, "where your treasure is, there will your heart be also" (Luke 12:34).

Everyone has their own 'gospel'. Everyone has the thing they wish to speak about and persuade others about. If we listen to what people talk about, then we can hear their true concerns.

The mouth will speak about what the heart values. If our hearts are directed towards earthly treasures, so our mouths will speak about these earthly realities. On the other hand, if our hearts are directed towards the kingdom of God, then our mouths will speak of this heavenly reality. And, perhaps rather strangely to our ears, speaking about this heavenly reality is also the key to radically transforming life in this world.

The risen Christ has launched his proclamation on the world, and now it is the time for proclamation. But what is the message that is being proclaimed in these last days?

Investigate

Re-read the following passages. What do they reveal about the *content* of the proclamation?

Luke 24:25-27

Luke 24:44-48

The message of redemption

Luke's birth narratives (Luke 1-2) overflow with joy at the angel's announcement of the coming of John and Jesus, and then at their births. There is a sense that the long-awaited time of redemption has at last arrived.

Redemption is a familiar Old Testament concept. The ancient Israelites were redeemed from slavery in Egypt. They were slaves, and they were set free by God's saving power. This rescue involved the conquest of the Egyptians and their gods, as well as God's provision of the Passover sacrifice, whose blood kept the Israelites safe so that they would not lose their firstborn and so that they could go free. It involved the exodus, the Old Testament's greatest miracle, when God parted the Red Sea and his people went through on dry ground. It involved God bringing his rescued people to their own promised land, where they would eventually enjoy rest.

When it was time for Jesus to be born, Zechariah prophesied, "the Lord … has visited and redeemed his people" (Luke 1:68). Later, on the mountain of transfiguration, Jesus spoke with his heavenly visitors, Moses and Elijah, about the "exodus" (Luke 9:31; ESV: "departure") that he was about to accomplish in Jerusalem. But when he eventually got to Jerusalem, he was crucified. What kind of a victory was that? The two disciples on the road to Emmaus were disappointed. "But we had hoped that he was the one to redeem Israel" (Luke 24:21). Jesus then corrected their perceptions. Presumably this means that he was, in fact, the one who would redeem Israel.

Why was this redemption necessary? What kind of slavery are human beings subject to?

Investigate

Read the following verses. What do they tell us about the state of the world?

Luke 3:3-9

Luke 10:17-20 (cf. Luke 4:5-7)

Luke 19:10

Acts 17:22-31

The kingdom of God

Human sinfulness has resulted in a lost world. Both Jew and Gentile have become, like the lost son (Luke 15:11-32), in "a far country"—that is, a long way away from God. In Jesus Christ, God himself mounts a rescue mission. "For the Son of Man came to seek and to save the lost" (Luke 19:10). This purpose of Jesus to "save" is seen time and again in the story, perhaps most famously in the parables of Luke 15, where the lost sheep, the lost coin and the lost son all speak of the same message: there is "joy in heaven over one sinner who repents" (Luke 15:7).

The parable of the lost son paints an even blacker picture. The fact of being away in a far country, and of being "lost", is also paralleled with being "dead" (Luke 15:24, 32). This, too, is a profound picture of the situation that our sinfulness has landed us in. We now live "in the shadow of death" (Luke 1:79). We need redemption from the shadow of death that dominates humanity's horizon. We need salvation from the grave.

The prophet Daniel had promised a great day of resurrection (Dan 12:1-2). The book of Daniel had spoken of the time when God would bring his own kingdom, as a replacement for all oppressive, bloodthirsty, ungodly human kingdoms (Dan 2:44). This kingdom of God would do away with the kind of wicked power that we know so tragically from the pages of human history. The vision of Daniel 7 showed that human kingdoms are just like 'beasts'. In the midst of this vision, Daniel saw "one like a son of man" coming on the clouds to the Ancient of Days, and he is then given the kingdom of God to reign over. By the end of the chapter, the suffering people of God are pictured as sharing in the kingdom ruled by the Son of Man. By the end of the book, this kingdom of God is, presumably, entered into by the resurrection from the dead.

Jesus regularly referred to himself as the Son of Man. It is no surprise, therefore, that he also spoke of the coming kingdom of God, and of resurrection.

Investigate

What is this message about the kingdom?

Luke 4:16-21, then 4:43-44

Luke 11:17-20[1]

1. Note that the meaning of "has come upon you" has created a lot of discussion. Since the kingdom of God is something to arrive in the future, Jesus is probably saying that his ministry has brought the kingdom of God ever so close; in fact, it is the very next thing to arrive in this world.

Luke 18:18-30

Luke 22:24-30

Luke 23:39-43

Acts 3:17-26

Acts 17:30-31

Acts 24:20-21, 24-26

Jesus: According to the Scriptures

Jesus has the key role in the coming of the future kingdom of God. It is no surprise, therefore, that the focus of the Gospel of Luke and the book of Acts, each in their own way, is on Jesus—who he is and what he did for us. To understand him properly, we have to understand God's plans and purposes revealed in the Old Testament Scriptures. From the beginning of his ministry, Jesus spoke of himself as fulfilling the Scriptures (Luke 4:16-21; cf. 24:25-27, 44-47).

As the early days of the apostolic preaching unfolded, their focus was clearly upon this man, who had been raised from the dead. Who was he? Why had he not stayed dead like the rest of the departed before him? What did his resurrection say about who he was and what he had achieved in the past—and what he would achieve in the future?

Investigate

1. Who is this risen one? And what has he achieved?

   Acts 2:22-36

   Acts 10:35-45

   Acts 3:17-26

   Acts 13:26-39

   Acts 17:29-31

2. Summarize the presentation of Jesus Christ in the early preaching.
   Jesus Christ is…

The proclamation of Jesus Christ today

The risen Christ launched his mission to the nations some two thousand years ago. As we believe the gospel, we speak it from a heart that is transformed. The message is the same, even if our world has greatly changed in some respects. However, in many other important respects, the world is exactly the same, and it is the same message that speaks to our world's greatest needs.

Think it through

1. What are some of the current views that people of today hold about Jesus Christ?

2. What are the points of contact between the early preaching about Jesus, and our contemporary hearers?

3. What are some of the current views about the future? How does the preaching of the kingdom of God answer these views?

4 Responding to the proclamation

When Jesus launched his mission to the nations, he was clear about the message and clear about the desired response: "... repentance and forgiveness of sins should be proclaimed in his name to all nations, beginning from Jerusalem" (Luke 24:47). Repentance: a turning to God (Acts 20:21; 26:20; see also 1 Thess 1:9-10)—for both Jew and Gentile. Repentance: a change of mind, a change of direction, a change of life. Perhaps, for the Jew (those in Jerusalem), this would mean one set of changes, for the Gentile (those amongst the nations), another set of changes. But for all, the one response: repentance.

Repentance as a change of mind about security

John the Baptist prepared the way for Jesus' gift of forgiveness. His baptism was preparatory, asking for repentance 'with a view to' the arrival of forgiveness with Jesus (Luke 3:3, 8; Acts 13:24; 19:4). When he arrived, Jesus likened himself to a doctor who moved amongst the sick; he did this because he had come to call sinners to repentance (Luke 5:31-32). So, what he would do as the risen Christ, he also did in his pre-resurrection mission to Israel. Evidently, this 'repentance' is the key response that Jesus calls for. But what is repentance, and what does it look like?

We need to avoid the fairly common 'moralistic' approach to repentance, which explains repentance as 'turning away from bad actions' (or some such definition). On this view, we *commit sins* and repentance means *feeling sorry*, and *turning away from those sins*. The 'New Year's resolution' might be an example of this kind of 'repentance'. The idea of 'doing penance' is also related to this understanding. But, even before we begin to look at some texts from Luke and Acts, it is important to realize that God doesn't deal with us 'on the surface'. The human problem is a deep, deep problem, which, as Jesus put it, goes right down to 'the heart' (Luke 6:43-46; cf. Mark 7:14-23).

John the Baptist prepared people for the arrival of the forgiveness of sins on a grand scale—long awaited by the prophets (Isa 40:1-2), pregnant with the expectation of a whole new creation (Isa 65-66). Jesus' first synagogue sermon picked up the Old Testament hopes (Luke 4:16-21; cf. Isa 61) and so his ministry, too, promised great things. The 'forgiveness for the prisoners' (Luke 4:18, literally) that he would bring, would issue in a whole new creation, the glorious kingdom of God (cf. Luke 4:43-44)! If Jesus' forgiveness was set upon such a grand scale, then we expect to find, and we do find, that his understanding of repentance is also going to be something on a grand scale. We must not trivialize repentance along moralistic lines.

Investigate

Try to build up a description of repentance from the following verses. Remember to keep an eye on 'the grand scale'.

Luke 3:7-14

Luke 10:8-23

Luke 12:22-34

Luke 14:17-20, 25-27

Luke 18:18-29

Life in this world under the shadow of death is a precarious existence. Where can we find a secure place in which to stand? The things that this world offers us promise to give the security we need. The more we own and the more people we are connected to, the more we can feel falsely at home and secure in this world. Repentance is to see things differently. Repentance is a change of heart, from a focus on and valuing of the things of this world, to a focus on and a valuing of the things of God's new world, the kingdom of God (Luke 12:34). This *re-valuation* of life leads to multiple and radical changes from the small details to the overall direction of our lives.

How does this radical re-orientation of life come about? It is not like a New Year's resolution, in which we simply decide for a change. Once again, when it comes to true repentance, something on the grand scale takes place.

Investigate

1. According to Luke 10:21-24, what causes repentance?

2. According to Luke 15:1-7 and 8-10, what brings a person to repentance? (Cf. Luke 19:10)

3. What is it about God that moves a person towards him? Can you find an answer in the famous parable of the lost son (Luke 15:11-32)?

When the Son of Man arrived in the world "to seek and to save the lost" (Luke 19:10), this was the great movement of God to bring his *grace* to this lost world. God had revealed himself in many and various ways in the past, but here was the great climax. And here, in this great climax of his self-revelation, he reveals himself to be the God of grace and mercy. His self-revelation draws us towards him. From our side, that is repentance.

Repentance as a change of mind about Jesus Christ

We also need to understand that repentance is thoroughly Christ-focused. John's baptism of repentance was a Christ-centred repentance (Luke 3:3, 8; Acts 13:24, 19:4). It was focused upon Jesus because it prepared the way for his coming and the forgiveness of sins. A person who came to John would have to believe in the (to them) future coming of Jesus, and, as a result of that belief in a promised future, they would repent. In Jesus' ministry, he called people to follow him in a radical way: leaving all the security structures of this world in order to follow him into the next (Luke 14:25-33). In other words, he was asking people to stake their present and future lives *on him*. He was asking them to trust him with their lives. What he was really after was faith (cf. Luke 18:8)—that is, faith *in him*.

Luke's entire Gospel is written to produce this kind of security in his readers (Luke 1:4). The resurrection of Jesus also provides this security in Jesus (Acts 2:36). To know Jesus Christ is to find a secure place in which to stand.

During his ministry, it wasn't easy to trust him with this kind of 'grand-scale' security in mind. After all, he seemed to be just a man, like the rest of us (cf. Luke 4:22-24).

As time went on, it would become even more difficult to trust him. When he arrived in Jerusalem, Jew and Gentile condemned him alike. The High Priests and their governing council (the duly appointed representatives of the Jewish people) joined forces with Pontius Pilate (the duly appointed representative of Rome), and this deadly coalition condemned Jesus to be crucified (Luke 23). Later, the early Christians saw that something on the grand scale was happening here. This was what Psalm 2 had spoken about—the great cosmic battle between humanity and the living God (see Acts 4:23-27). The representatives of both Jew and Gentile had crucified Jesus, and he was God's appointed king. A big mistake had been made.

When Jesus rose from the dead, this was God overturning the judgement that we human beings had passed on Jesus. The resurrection calls for a re-assessment of the human decision about Jesus—killing him exposes our deep, deep sinfulness. The resurrection calls for a re-assessment of Jesus. He was innocent, not guilty, and we were the guilty ones. It calls for a re-assessment of his scandalous death on the cross—the scandal he bore was not for him—it was for us. This re-assessment is at the core of repentance.

Investigate

What re-assessment did the resurrection of Jesus call for?

Acts 2:22-24, 30-31, 36

Acts 3:13-26

Acts 4:29-32

Note: To be hanged on a tree was a sign of being under the curse of God (Deut 21:22). Jesus died under the curse of God, but the resurrection forces a reassessment: he bore the curse for us! See Galatians 3:13-14.

Repentance is the reception of God's grace that is found in his Son, who "loved me and gave himself for me" (Gal 2:20). The risen Lord, through his apostles, issues the call to repentance to the entire world, both Jew and Gentile. As Paul put it, he had testified "both to Jews and to Greeks of repentance toward God and of faith in our Lord Jesus Christ" (Acts 20:21). A turning to God—to his new world, to his wonderful grace that he alone reveals, and to a life lived by faith in Jesus Christ, who died for us, and then rose again on our behalf.

This kind of repentance is radical. It is life changing from the core to the surface.

Change of mind, change of life

Repentance leads to a change of life. Even John's preparatory baptism asked for the baptized to bear fruit that showed their repentance (Luke 3:8). When Paul was converted and called to be the apostle to the Gentiles, he preached to the Gentiles that "they should repent and turn to God, performing deeds in keeping with their repentance" (Acts 26:20).

Repentance begins with the recognition that God has been gracious towards us in Jesus Christ (cf. Luke 15:17). If God has been gracious towards us, then this means that we are lost without him (see Luke 15:11-21). Repentance begins with this double recognition at one and the same time, that God is gracious—therefore we must be lost. Our eyes are opened, and we see the light of God (Acts 26:17-18). This change of sight and change of heart leads to a turning around and a change of life. We can never be the same again.

Think it through

1. What prevents us from grasping the depth and breadth of repentance?

2. What is the most radical thing that you have learned about repentance?

3. If radical repentance is to be seen in our lost and dying world, what is the 'secret' that will need to get out?

4. What will true Christian repentance look like?

5 Blessings from the proclamation

If the world is lost, and the kingdom of God—with resurrection, judgement and eternal life—is just around the corner, what will happen to the world? There is clearly a need for salvation. But if our lost state is caused by human sinfulness, then this needs to be dealt with as well.

This is why the risen Christ announces that the proclamation of the gospel centres on forgiveness. "Thus it is written, that the Christ should suffer and on the third day rise from the dead, and that repentance and forgiveness of sins should be proclaimed in his name to all nations, beginning from Jerusalem" (Luke 24:46-47). We should also notice that these three items are all drawn from the Scriptures, according to Jesus' exposition.

Investigate

1. What do these verses have in common (not in regard to the detail, but in regard to the general approach)?

   Luke 4:20-21; 24:25-27, 32, 44-47

   Acts 2:15-21, 24-25, 34-35; 8:30-35; 10:43; 13:32-37

2. What is the effect of explaining Jesus in the light of 'the Scriptures'?

God has been working in his world from the beginning. He has revealed his plans and purposes by various means in the past, as recorded in the Scriptures, and his self-revelation comes to a grand climax in his Son. There is enormous strength in recognizing that the Christian faith is grounded in God's self-revelation in history and goes back to his plans in eternity (cf. Titus 1:2). It is part of what produces the tremendous sense of security that is found in the Christian life.

Forgiveness leads to security

We have already noticed in the last study that 'repentance' means turning to find your security in the living God and in his promises of eternal life. Believing God's promises for the future then revolutionizes life in the present world. Forgiveness of sins is the key in this revolutionary, transformation-bringing process!

When the risen Christ launched his mission to the nations, it was centred on the proclamation of the forgiveness of sins (Luke 24:47; cf. Acts 10:43).

Investigate

1. According to the following verses, what good things are associated with the forgiveness of sins?

   Luke 1:77-79

Luke 3:3-6

Luke 4:17-19

Acts 2:37-40 (cf. v. 21)

Acts 5:29-32

Acts 13:37-48

Acts 26:15-18

2. How do these things transform all of life?

3. How do these things bring the security, assurance, and confidence that Luke aims at for his readers (cf. Luke 1:4)?

Forgiveness leads to proclamation

The word about forgiveness being available in Jesus Christ is a thoroughly revolutionary word. Jesus launched this word on a world in great need of it. Whenever it is believed, it seems to bubble up from the depths of a person's heart, and come out of their mouth in the form of good news for the *next* person. Notice how this seems to have happened in the early days.

Investigate

What is the response to forgiveness? Why does it happen this way?

Luke 7:36-50

Acts 2:37-41

Acts 2:42-47

Acts 4:32-35

Acts 17:1-9; see also 1 Thessalonians 1:5-10

Acts 17:32-33

This revolutionary word about forgiveness spread and spread throughout the ancient world. Within a very brief period it had "turned the world upside down" (according to one of its opponents—see Acts 17:6). It spread like wildfire across the Roman world, and, in time, it radically changed human society and the face of human history. Now *that* is truly a word of power.

Think it through

Luke wrote his gospel so that his readers might find security, or "certainty", in the things of Jesus (see Luke 1:4). On the day of Pentecost, Peter said that the message about Jesus' resurrection could also be known with security, or "for certain" (Acts 2:36).

1. Can you point to signs of a deep anxiety in our contemporary world?

2. How does the security found in Christ's message of forgiveness *speak* to the anxiety in our world?

3. How does the security that arises from forgiveness in Christ help with your own anxieties?

4. How does this security in Christ relate to Jesus' mission to a lost world into which we have been caught up?

6 Progress of the proclamation

As we look back on the beginnings of the time of proclamation, the first century seems to be such a long time ago, and the land of Israel such a long way away. Culturally, the contemporary world seems to be almost on another planet from the one in which Jesus was put to death on a cross, and in which he rose again from the dead. We have come a long way.

But, even though we look back in time and space and culture, when we look back on those beginnings, it is like gazing on a family tree. This is our heritage. The proclamation that began way back then, has even reached *to us*. Where will it go now? What will the regions beyond us look like?

Investigate

Read Luke 24:45-48 and Acts 1:8.

1. What progress for the gospel does Jesus chart?

2. Why must the gospel progress in this way? Answer from the following passages:

   Luke 2:28-32

Acts 4:23-31 (see especially Psalm 2:8)

Acts 10:34-43

The apostolic *witness*

Sometimes the apostles are referred to by the shorthand term, 'the first Christians'. Although this is absolutely correct, it is potentially misleading. For the apostles were much more than the first Christians. They were Jesus' chosen and appointed *witnesses.*

Investigate

For each of the following passages, list the *language* that speaks of eyewitness testimony, and notice what *results from* eyewitness testimony.

Luke 1:1-4

Luke 2:8-20

Luke 8:26-39

Luke 24:36-48

It is often said in common Christian speech that Christians are 'witnesses' to Christ. This is certainly true in the sense that we all have a story to tell of how Christ has transformed our lives as a result of our faith in him. In some circles it is common in Church meetings to have a congregation member give a 'testimony' (i.e. an act of witness), which usually consists of them telling how they were converted, or what Christ is doing in their life right now.

We must remember, however, that this is a loose use of the word 'witness'. Or, to put it another way, it is not using the language of 'witness' and 'testimony' in exactly the same way that the New Testament does. In the New Testament it is a *technical term*. The 'witness' family draws upon the setting of the law court. Just like today's legal system, the ancient legal system relied upon collecting evidence from the testimony of those who had seen, heard, and touched the events of interest to the court. The courts sought to establish the truth, by relying upon *eyewitness testimony*. These people are the only people who can actually say what went on. Everyone else is dependent upon the testimony of the eyewitnesses for any access to the truth of what happened.

This is the normal way in which information and knowledge is accumulated in our world. We cannot experience everything. The vast majority of our knowledge is based on reports that date back to those who *actually knew*, that is, the eyewitnesses.

In writing his Gospel, Luke was careful to check his facts and to report only what the eyewitnesses spoke about (see Luke 1:1-4). This enables his readers to know for certain that his story about Jesus is true. Here is the grounds for security.

It is one of the wonderful features of God's grace and kindness that he communicates *his* truth, through the same processes that we are used to using in everyday, normal human life. God uses *eyewitness testimony*.

The *apostolic* witness

This means that everyone who wishes to understand God's plans and purposes for his world is absolutely dependent upon those who saw, heard, and touched the evidence. To ensure that this witness continued for all time, Jesus took special steps to establish and commission a group of specially appointed witnesses. These are his 'apostles', that is, according to the meaning of the word, his 'sent ones'.

Investigate

1. How do the following passages show the *specialness* of the apostles?

   Luke 1:1-4

   Luke 24:36-49

   Acts 1:15-26

   Acts 10:39-43

   Acts 13:30-31

2. Summarize:
   The apostles are important for the future of Christianity because…

When Jesus gathered with his chosen apostles in the upper room after he rose from the dead, there was still one apostle yet to be appointed (after Matthias, the replacement for Judas). In order for the gospel to go out to the Gentiles—that is, the nations other than the Jewish people—Jesus commissioned perhaps the most surprising of all his apostles. Saul the persecutor, as the famous story tells us, was stopped in his tracks in the midst of his persecution of the fledgling Christian movement, and he eventually became Paul, the apostle to the Gentiles (see Acts 9; 22:1-21; 26:1-18). Paul then embarked upon the mission to the nations of the world that would consume his every waking hour until the end of his days.

Paul was well aware that he was *not* one of the original, *foundational* apostles. He knew that they had a special role, especially in relation to the Jewish people (Acts 13:30-31). He could not witness to exactly the same things that they could, because he did not share the same eyewitness experience of Jesus' ministry from John the Baptist to the crucifixion. Paul was also aware, however, that his authority as an apostle was not at all diminished. He was called to witness to the things that he both saw and heard (see Acts 26:16-18). That is, he had encountered the risen Lord, who had then commissioned him for the special task of being the apostle to the Gentiles (cf. Gal 1; 1 Cor 9:1, 15:1-8). The twelve took the message to the Jews. Paul brought the same message to the Gentile nations of the world. They all spoke the same apostolic word.

The apostolic word

The apostolic word is not simply the collected thoughts of the first Christians concerning God. It is not as if their word is on the same level as *our* thoughts about God. Nor is the New Testament (which is the apostolic word written down) simply a record of what first-century Christians thought about God. Often those who take such a view will then go on to say that it is up to every new generation of Christians to have their own thoughts about God. Some of the things that are found in the New Testament, on this view, are outdated and outmoded and should be updated and upmoded! This updating process is only permissible, or even essential, because of the belief that the apostles' word has no more authority that our own thoughts about God.

But this is seriously mistaken. The thing about eyewitness testimony is that it stands for all time. It cannot be outdated or outmoded. It is nonsense to say it can be updated and upmoded. Present day Christians were not at the right place and the right time to know the truth. It is only those who were, and those who were specially commissioned for this task, who have the authority to speak of the things that God has done on behalf of the world. Their eyewitness testimony and the teaching based upon it, stands for all people, for all time. That is the nature of the beast. They gave the world a gift: the 'apostolic deposit'. This 'deposit' must be passed on from generation to generation.

Investigate

1. What do the following passages show about the apostolic deposit?

   2 Timothy 1:9b-14; 2:1-2; 4:1-5.
   Note the different translation of 1:12b in the ESV footnote.

   Luke 1:1-4

   Luke 24:44-49

   Acts 1:1-8

2. The book of Acts actually records many 'summaries' of the apostolic teaching. Given what we have seen about 'the apostolic deposit', what role do you think these summaries have for future generations?

Apostolic *unity*, for the sake of mission

There has always been a lot of talk of unity in Christian circles. Just like God is Father, Son and Spirit in perfect unity, Christian people are also called to be united together. This call to unity has often been issued in the context of mission. 'If we want to reach out to the world, then we ought to be united in Christ.'

But unfortunately, the most basic kind of unity that leads to true interpersonal unity is often neglected in such discussions. True Christian unity is not the kind of artificial unity that decides to 'beg to differ', or to tolerate all kinds of diverse opinions and persuasions in order to give the appearance of a household in order. It is not the kind of artificial unity that is based on denominational loyalties, or institutions, or resolutions, or other such human structures. The kind of unity that is true Christian unity is *God's* kind of unity.

This means that true unity is a unity that is grounded in and built by a unity *in the apostolic faith*—through accepting and believing their eyewitness testimony about the risen Christ, and through accepting and believing and living the teaching that they give based on that greatest of all events. It is only unity with the apostles that enables unity with Christ himself and through Christ with the living God (see John 17:20-23).

A false kind of unity can be attempted in any number of ways. But there is no true unity without apostolic unity. When the apostolic tradition is dispensed with, this is the source of 'schism', for a departure from the apostolic word is a departure from Christ himself (who commissioned his witnesses) and so from Christ's church.

Christian tradition does not *develop* over time. It is, as Jude put it, "once for all *delivered* to the saints" (Jude 3). Luke, for his part, records this deposit in two halves: firstly in his Gospel, and secondly in the book of Acts. This means that future generations, including our own, have the wonderful privilege and responsibility to pass this deposit on to our generation. We can relax—there is no need to re-invent the message; there is no need to try to be clever enough to understand what the world *really* needs to hear (!). God has already done all that. He has done something in human history that stands for all people for all time. All we need to do is to listen to the apostolic word, believe it, repeat it, and keep on repeating it. This deposit never changes. It has no need to. It is always just what the world needs; just what the doctor ordered (see Luke 5:31-32).

As we speak the apostle's word to our generation, God will work through it, for it is the word of the risen Christ, and he will continue his mission, even unto the end of the age.

Think it through

1. Why will the gospel keep progressing? (Think back over all the various studies that you have done during these last weeks.)

2. What is the importance of the preservation and repetition of the 'apostolic deposit'? What will become of Christ's mission if this preservation and repetition is not faithfully passed on?

3. If the proclamation will keep progressing, where are some "fields that are white for harvest" (John 4:35) in your little part of the world? Think about what will have to happen for the gospel to progress into these new 'fields'.

4. If the proclamation will keep progressing, where are some “fields that are white for harvest” around your church? Think about what will have to happen for the gospel to progress into these new ‘fields’.

5. If the proclamation will keep progressing, where are some “fields that are white for harvest” at some distance from your part of the world or your church? Think about what will have to happen for the gospel to progress into these new ‘fields’.

Who are we?

Ever since we opened our doors in 1991 in the UK as St Matthias Press, our aim has been to provide the Christian community with products of a uniformly high standard–both in their biblical faithfulness and in the quality of the writing and production.

Now known as **The Good Book Company,** we have grown together with our Australian partner **Matthias Media** become an international provider of user-friendly resources, with Christians of all sorts using our Bible studies, books, Briefings, audio cassettes, videos, training courses and events.

Buy direct from us and save

If you order your resources direct from us, you can not only save time and money, you invest in more great resources for the future:

- you save time–we usually despatch our orders within 24 hours of receiving them
- you save money–if you order in bulk, you'll save even more
- you help keep us afloat–because we get more from each sale, buying from us direct helps us to stay alive and develop new Biblical resources for the future.

Please call us for a free catalogue of all our resources, including an up-to-date list of other titles in this Interactive Bible Studies series. Some details of IBS titles are contained on the following page.

Phone	Post	FAX
0845 225 0880	Elm House, 37 Elm Road, New Malden, Surrey KT3 3HB	0845 225 0990 (pay by credit card or invoice)

Email: admin@thegoodbook.co.uk
Website: www.thegoodbook.co.uk

Interactive Bible studies

Our Interactive Bible studies (IBS) and Topical Bible Studies (TBS) are a valuable resource to help you keep feeding from God's Word. The IBS series works through passages and books of the Bible; the TBS series pulls together the Bible's teaching on topics, such as money or prayer. As of March 2005, the series contains the following 30 titles. Call us or visit the website for the most up-to-date listing. 0845 225 0880; www.thegoodbook.co.uk

OLD TESTAMENT

FULL OF PROMISE (THE BIG PICTURE OF THE O.T.)
Authors: Phil Campbell & Bryson Smith, 8 studies

BEYOND EDEN (GENESIS 1-11)
Authors: Phillip Jensen and Tony Payne, 9 studies

THE ONE AND ONLY (DEUT)
Author: Bryson Smith, 8 studies

THE GOOD, THE BAD & THE UGLY (JUDGES)
Author: Mark Baddeley, 10 studies

FAMINE & FORTUNE (RUTH)
Authors: Barry Webb & David Hohne, 4 studies

THE EYE OF THE STORM (JOB)
Author: Bryson Smith, 6 studies

THE SEARCH FOR MEANING (ECCLESIASTES)
Author: Tim McMahon, 9 studies

TWO CITIES (ISAIAH)
Authors: Andrew Reid and Karen Morris, 9 studies

KINGDOM OF DREAMS (DANIEL)
Authors: Andrew Reid and Karen Morris, 8 studies

RENOVATOR'S DREAM (NEH)
Phil Campbell & Greg Clarke, 7 studies

WARNING SIGNS (JONAH)
Author: Andrew Reid, 6 studies

BURNING DESIRE (OBADIAH & MALACHI)
Authors: Phillip Jensen and Richard Pulley, 6 studies

NEW TESTAMENT

THE GOOD LIVING GUIDE (MATTHEW 5:1-12)
Authors: Phillip Jensen and Tony Payne, 9 studies

NEWS OF THE HOUR (MARK)
Author: Peter Bolt, 10 studies

FREE FOR ALL (GALATIANS)
Authors: Phillip Jensen & Kel Richards, 8 studies

WALK THIS WAY (EPHESIANS)
Author: Bryson Smith, 8 studies

PARTNERS FOR LIFE (PHILIPPIANS)
Author: Tim Thorburn, 8 studies

THE COMPLETE CHRISTIAN (COLOSSIANS)
Authors: Phillip Jensen and Tony Payne, 8 studies

ALL LIFE IS HERE (1 TIMOTHY)
Authors: Phillip Jensen and Greg Clarke, 9 studies

RUN THE RACE (2 TIMOTHY)
Author: Bryson Smith, 6 studies

THE PATH TO GODLINESS (TITUS)
Authors: Phillip Jensen and Tony Payne, 6 studies

FROM SHADOW TO REALITY (HEBREWS)
Author: Joshua Ng, 10 studies

THE IMPLANTED WORD (JAMES)
Authors: Phillip Jensen and K.R. Birkett, 8 studies

HOMEWARD BOUND (1 PETER)
Authors: Phillip Jensen and Tony Payne, 10 studies

ALL YOU NEED TO KNOW (2 PETER)
Author: Bryson Smith, 6 studies

THE VISION STATEMENT (REVELATION)
Author: Greg Clarke, 9 studies

TOPICAL BIBLE STUDIES

BOLD I APPROACH (PRAYER)
Author: Tony Payne, 6 studies

CASH VALUES (MONEY)
Author: Tony Payne, 5 studies

THE BLUEPRINT (DOCTRINE)
Authors: Phillip Jensen & Tony Payne, 11 studies

WOMAN OF GOD (THE BIBLE ON WOMEN)
Author: Terry Blowes, 8 studies

Two ways to live: Know and share the gospel

The *Two ways to live* training course stems from the conviction that every Christian should know and understand the gospel clearly for themselves, and be able to explain their faith simply and clearly when the opportunity arises.

Knowing the gospel leads inevitably to telling the gospel. How we do so will, of course, depend on our particular abilities, circumstances and opportunities. This course does not assume that every Christian will have the same gifts and opportunities to share the gospel.

Participants spend some time looking at what the Bible says about sharing the gospel, and at the attitudes, motivations and methods that should accompany it. Then, they learn how to use the *Two ways to live* outline to share the gospel with others. This involves learning to adapt the basic outline to their own natural patterns of speech, and practising this skill in different contexts.

Course materials

i. Participant's Manual–each person doing the course needs one of these, including the leader. It includes an enhanced audio CD containing two talks on the logic of the gospel, plus other multimedia resources to help in learning the *Two ways to live* outline.

ii. Leader's Manual–this contains an extensive introduction to the rationale, aims and methods of the course, how to set up the training in our church or fellowship, as well as comprehensive notes, tips and content to enable you to lead each session.

iii. Training Video/DVD–this contains a range of very useful role plays and demonstrations that help participants see different facets of *Two ways to live* in action. It also contains extra information and input for the leader about this course.

FOR MORE INFORMATION OR TO ORDER CONTACT:

United Kingdom
The Good Book Company
Telephone: 0845 225 0880
Facsimile: 0845 225 0990
Email: admin@thegoodbook.co.uk

www.thegoodbook.co.uk